no apologies

Some of these poems have appeared
in Big Mama Rag, Black Maria, Brim,
Cathartic, Connections, Moving Out,
Off Our Backs, Stone, The Boston
Phoenix, TCB, Women Writing.

Design: Stephanie Mauer

Photography and drawings: Polly Joan
Barbara Anger: "muscle"
Paul Gibbons: "Polly Joan on Mt. Jefferson"

Glad Day Press
UNION SHOP I.U.
450
308 Stewart Ave., Ithaca, N.Y. 14850

polly joan
no apologies

WOMEN WRITING PRESS
NEW YORK

for my mom

Alice Katherine
from Amherst, Ohio

No Apologies

have you ever asked yourself
why the statistics for less
incidence of heart failure
in women
could have a medical base

so far not put forth
by scientists who
criticize their wives
for being too / emotional

a muscle atrophies
w/disuse
rationally placidly
insisting the same sane
two tears
quickly brushed aside
dead sons or new daughters

no wonder hearts fail
on a snow shovel

a woman constantly constricts
adapts expands defends
keeps in physical shape
a feeling/muscle

no more apologies
for my healthy heart
no more apologies
for being a typical / woman

I am very happily / pumping
to every / emotional / cell

The Last Poem

Shall I try once more
to tell you about the circus?

The breasted freaks
The candied apples
Carmel-coated and skewered
Turned upside down on trays
Waiting to be sold

Shall I tell you about clowns?
Jumping in and out of their pants
Pratt falls for a pop gun
Caricatures for emotions
Competing for your laughter

Shall I tell you about darkness?
About empty seats and candy wrappers
About cotton candy tubes
And half-eaten hot dogs
And crushed popcorn in the dirt

Shall I tell you again
again again

After Eighteen Years

is our love hanging
    on a branch of dying Elm
suckling on raspberries
    in dead winter
reaching for kittens
    over the body of an old cat

I wonder

cold
vacant
stare
why the robins are late

the grass is nothing
brown
the suet cake is finished
are we

3 AM
Walking In The Field

My impaled womb
   is bearable

judged
   no more

The moon
   is not a god

Her light
   asks no candles

Elm Tree

She is dead
I am not

Her arms stretch out
like mad women
in a snake pit
yet she is not a skeleton
I want to forget

She is beautiful as I am
with my crooked arms
and twisted roots

Her world hit her and loved her
Her leaves finally curled
into helpless little fists
and fell

She still stands

Dear Byron

"Disguise ev'n tenderness if thou art wise
Brisk Confidence still best with woman copes:
Pique her and soothe in turn, soon Passion
                    crowns they hopes"   Byron

No longer can he beguile her
to writhe in his marketplace
a showpiece for his friends
a willing dancer for his ego

No longer will she crumple
peacefully into her basket

The queen cobra barred her head for a lute
She forgot her bite
She forgot

She was a snake

It was easier
    to think of him as Sir Galahad
He rode his image well
    Comfortable Confident Controlled

She waved him off to many a quest
    sewing philosophy
into lonely hours

Now

He sits in his room
    wrapped in justice
glaring out of tarnished tin
    misplaced

It is a pity
    but she has none
She shot his horse

Being Honest With People Can Be Lonely

I am not sure
I can keep
spilling my blood

to be stepped on
no less bloodlessly
because a knife
is not used

Am I really insensitive

Deluding my sense of Self?

Do I stick a blade
all unknowingly

into the vulva
of another frightened
rabbit?

Am I rejected because
somewhere I have become a stone
that knows only how to cut

to strike back
because of my own smelly sores?

I mistrust who I am
what I think I have discovered

of love

and loving

I reach for my fig leaves
pocketing my open palms
in the earth's dirt

I bury myself
not wishing to die

Changes

I am not even pretty anymore.
My face is soapstone and yellowed.
I would not mind my aging
if my lines were soft
like I wanted to be,
but I am carved into
permanent sadness.
My face has become hard
to survive being soft
while you, my flower man,
grow softer every day.
You look brushed with
pink powder and health.

    I hate your face
    I hate your softness

because you are becoming feminine
and you will be applauded
while I, who was born soft,
have evolved into the
Old Man of the White Mountains.

On Remaining A Tulip

Have you ever seen a tulip
when it starts to die

when it rains
and the petals fall off
one by one

discolored
and wrinkled

It's hard to die
over and over again
so I'm tough

I only caress velvet
with nostalgia

the long ball gown
the entrance to the dance
my shoulders bare
glowing

Touch me now!

a bow string
equipped with arrows
taut gut
between two arms
my legs separated
by a pair of jeans

What will happen to society
if all the soft ones
have to become carnivours

wary
even when purring

blood for blood
or bleached bones enduring

Bury me not
away from the sun

I am a flower
and I will
survive

If I have no other choice
you will find

tulips

scratched
on the walls of the cave

Develop Your Self Image At The Gynecologist's

When I was 14
there was a big discussion
at my yearly checkup
about whether to inject
my breasts w/foam
my mother and the doctor
decided against it
because w/time
the stuff got crunchy
rice krispie breasts
they figured
was worse
than being
small
I wasn't
asked
for
my
opinion
I just lay w/my bare bottom
on the examining table
(they didn't use sheets
in those days for
adolescents)
getting colder
and colder
and colder
and littler
and littler
and littler

Scarred

I had a baby
   two babies
three
   I am not ugly

My mounds
   were bean hills growing
until
   the surface split
and they came

Cracks on my earth
   Glossy rivulets

Jewelry
   for my bikini

Re-Interpreting The Bible

Who said

>   When you grow up
>   Put away childish things?

Take sucking for example

Pure delight!
Wasted!

Perfectly marvelous
would be cocksuckers
breastsuckers
or what-ever-you-can-think-of-suckers
becoming very very adult
pencil chewers
beer bottle nursers
nail biters
pipe tasters
eye glass nibblers

while mothers become
hide and seek sucked suckers
enjoying their babies mouthes
at night

beautiful nights
(never mind 2 am)
rocking
being sucked
no one to see their pleasure
their smiles
their holes tingling
their sweet
dark orgies
into incest
otherwise known as
and socially accepted as
a "good start" for the child
making the child "secure"
satisfying the early childhood
sucking syndrome
a preventative for thumbsucking

Consciousness * Raising

I wonder
if the Black-eyed Susans
are wiser
than I

They keep tight-rooted
waving their yellow scarves at me
like cheerful housewives
on small town porches

I keep yanking
at my roots
until I flop
in the grass

Daughter

She brought me
     a blue china goose
bending her neck to her wings
That was my birthday

When I was sick
     she drew her happy people
and little poem
and left them on my pillow

Yesterday
     it was a silkscreened cat
grinning through orange paint
lying on the living room rug

I wonder gentle daughter
     always falling
from the branches of your willow
whether I

reaching so hard
     for my own liberation
have forgotten
how to give

15th Summer-Stump On The Strings

He was out on the driveway
first day of vacation
fixing
his wonderful machine
Finger painting his teeshirt
his blond hair hanging
intense face proud
as an Indian

Faulty gears at midday
slipping out of threads
an innocent link in a spinning chain
yanking off a finger

      My god Mom
      I play the guitar

Crawling over gravel
hands and knees shaking
dis-membered fingers
look like stones

Found Sewn back Held
over his heart
eight days odor
dying rat in the wall
little piece of my son
that wouldn't live

      I keep feeling
      the end Mom

Summer heat
browning the grass
no rain jet trails
across my Cherokee's eyes

      I'm healing it flat Mom
      to hold my pic

His will is water
shaping a rock
pink calloused stump
for his strings

Love Shouldn't Have To Play/God

There was a boy named Fredo
from East Harlem
who was Puerto Rican and poor
and beautiful
who
wanted to live w/us
be loved
He hated Chris
Chris was our son
We loved him / both Chris / Fredo
and he put a big
knife / to Chris' neck
I had dysentery for 2 months
I had to say no / to Fredo

Fredo
couldn't read
He didn't know why the moon
was round
He wanted to know
He didn't want to be a junkie
He wanted to get out / of East Harlem
I had to say no to Fredo
because I loved Chris
I loved Fredo

Bullets

I.   Crime is the result
    of powerlessness

    Murderers are only
    inverted suicides
    sanity enough left
    to know
    their selfhood
    isn't rotten

2.   Madness is another form
    of suicide

    It is made to order
    for any spiritual person
    believing in "after life"

    who chooses oblivion
    as a fool proof method
    for escape
    over the less certain permanence
    of death

3.   5 pm
    spasms / the world jerking
    rock / rock
    need heart / chair
    find the same rhythm
    keep me / sane
    keep me / sane
    keep me / sane
    keep me / sane

Victim Of A Witch Hunt

Ethel Rosenberg
her last
loving

Oh god
tortured words

leaving to her children
waiting for the electric chair

energy to kill energy
so vital it required
extra shocks
to kill

      The wooden chair blessed
      as a place

      for taking bread and strength
      and peace
      before sleep

How can I deal
with human distortion

the karma

of a simple chair?

On Being A Vegetable

I am shaped like a summer gourd.
I thought it was normal,
rather nice. He says
I am suited for a glossy pullout
in ORGANIC GARDENING

Is that bad?

I think I may dry up inside
until my seeds rattle
when he shakes me;
or else,
I will eat myself
into a horny warted squash.

It is amazing more women
don't expand into enormous pumpkins.
I have seen some. They stare
out of halloween masks
carved on their lined faces.
They don't look like women anymore.

October

She remembered the fall
she had stood in her garden
watching the geese

She had felt so betrayed

They were all escaping
They were all honking
They were all beautiful
They were all being true

to themselves

and she woke up in the night
when they returned

holding the sound in her ears

Why Is Everybody Staring ?

I am screaming
I am very loud
I am not sick
I do not need
a quiet corner
and "there there"

I do not need
any further training

On the contrary
I demand a bigger room
I want to hear me
echo

To Joan

Madness Is Part Of The Process

I want to hold her when she flies
screaming

I do not want her to
bang against the window

My arms make her angry
so long has she waited

She does not understand
how I honor
her madness

Appliqued on the headboard of her soft bed
out of love and for love
she embroidered on her flesh flowers
applauded
for keeping the needle
moving in and out of her skin

Her scream is a voice of truth
withdrawal her entry into conflict
madness recognized as madness
not disgraceful
not to be pitied
but unbearable
this loving of her Self

willfully destroying what she
carefully created cutting the stitches
ripping silk roses off of her
breast red threads torn velvet

I want to hold her when she flies
screaming

I want to accept her child
tuck her into a feather bed
leave the night light on
not make her need
ashamed

The window will not open
It is painted shut
She is right
She will have to break it

I want to see her
attack like a hawk
the calico hood removed
from her head
knowing she is not alone
grace and love listening
cheering and weeping with her
over sounds of smashing glass

Fragments

I.   Memo to Blake's TIGER

         I tiger
         my womanhood
         burning
         my symmetry immortal

         am
         unacceptable

2.   I grew behind the garage

         my bottom too big
         my breasts too small

     The wind touched me
     like my mother's hand
     then pulled back

         my body
         now a woman's

3.   Women have been napalmed
     by what they've missed
     They have to invent cures
     or remain ugly
     or remain ugly
     or go mad
     or die

4. Consciousness-raising
   for all its high billing
   doesn't usually
   bring a woman

   any peace

5. I sat on the roof
   begging the night
   for wings
   feeling the cold/marble/stumps
   under my nitie

   torn fly wings
   cannot be glued
   I tried

6. Memo to women

   Read Plath and Virginia Woolf
   Add / Anne Sexton

   Dead suicides
   can keep you
   alive
   they listen

Salem Witch

I see you hanging
Grandma Allen

Flung from the white church
into the twisted tree
I watch your Sunday shoes
kicking the air

Did the Great Father take your soul
when they cut the rope
or were you allowed to lie
in the belly of the goddess?

Easter Poem

I will speak to you of Love

The soldiers tore off my dress
and nailed me to a wooden frame
poked my nipples
stuck their fingers in my crotch
played games for my clothes
laughed and smelled my lace
panties
Peter lay hidden somewhere
in fear but my mother sat
before me
weeping strength into my dying
And later when no man dared
she came to my cold tomb
to touch my broken body
for the last time
And I knew the pain of my
coming and going
had killed her too
but she would stay alive
to raise my daughters

Brought Up On Jesus

I will tell you about the other Mary

who had no dowry
who was an outcast
who couldn't sell her baskets
who couldn't bring herself to beg
who finally spread her legs apart
and men took her

       threw her their pennies
       their dark guilt
       their spittle

their gentle daughters which she
aborted with a bone
burying the black sticky balls at night
her breasts flowing

She heard about a celibate priest
who spoke only of love
and she went to him
saw his pain and weariness
and washed his feet with her
hair and tears and tenderness

He looked at her on her knees
and raising his arms
he forgave her for her sins

That night the bone was not
for her cunt

but for her heart

Breakfast At Woolworth's

She came and sat across from me

    Don't I know you
    from somewhere?

She had seen my eyes before
but no
we had never met

Sip by sip
her stories fell
her cupped hands catching
each one
holding them out to me

It was because of Vietnam.
Her boyfriend didn't know.
He came back and well
she caught it you know.
They found out too late.
The disease is permanent.
Nothing lives. Laugh.
She is getting used to
miscarriages. All the time.
She just flushes the toliet.
Gone. Just like that.
If only they didn't have eyes.
You know they really do
have eyes. Laugh.

She wadded her napkin
pushed away her cup
It was time to go

flung a strap over her shoulder
shuffled out of Woolworths
leaving
all her babies
all her babies

This woman you find
in the sawdust
is real
hanging my door
not myself
in the opening

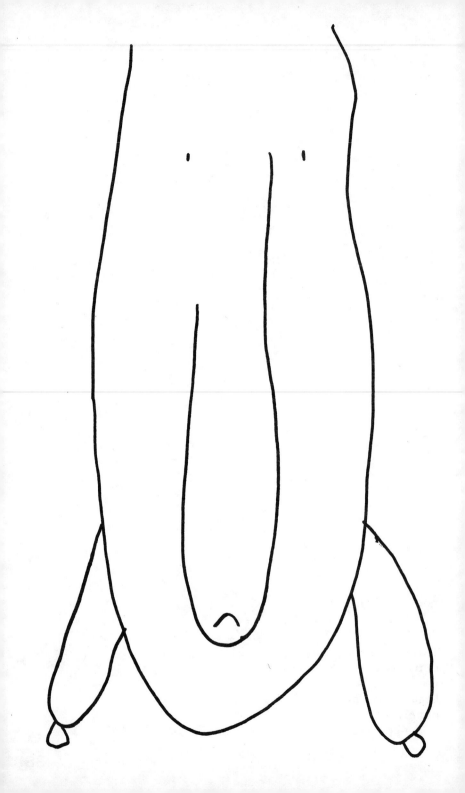

How Does Your Garden Grow ?

maybe you will find
me in the garden and we will
make love on warm
hay mulch your penis
hard as a zuccini wildly
growing giant could
take a hundred such
vegetables daily into
my round hot grassy
pot hole joy yes
why not yes
summer's coming oh
YES

Camping

Don't pee
    on the path said He

So I
    to satisfy His
    fastidious whim

must go clambering into the
    prickly brush

squatting like a toadstool

    while He
    All Lordly

squirts
    from where he stands

It is too easy
for a woman
to squat herself
right-out-of-sight

New Lifestyle

It is too bad we cannot
curl up with our books
bodies on the same couch
warming each other's
round rump
we study
what is wrong w/marriage
on / separate / chairs
we NEVER / ask
we ./ are independent
we / are alternative
we / COPE
we / are / re / learning
to suck / our own thumb
have / our / temper / tantrum
in our / own / room
share everything / with
al / ter / na / tives
next / door
It is called / OPEN MARRIAGE
published / 1972
Avon Books / division of the
Hearst / Corporation

Happiness Is A Big Muscle

A favorite game is comparing
muscles I before
only observer
now an active flexed
right arm
indian wrestling my sons
stronger than
late blooming mothers I
can still push over my
daughter on the kitchen floor
but she's only eleven damn it
and already
pressing forty

When I went to Stephanie's
for coffee she
wanted to move the trunk
herself   We quickly
stopped everything
rolled up our sleeves
her upper arm quite
impressive but my forearm
obviously incredible
didn't seem conclusive
so we whipped off our shirts did

a twin atlas job
in front of the mirror
so delightful
we ignored the trunk
and fixed a second cup of coffee

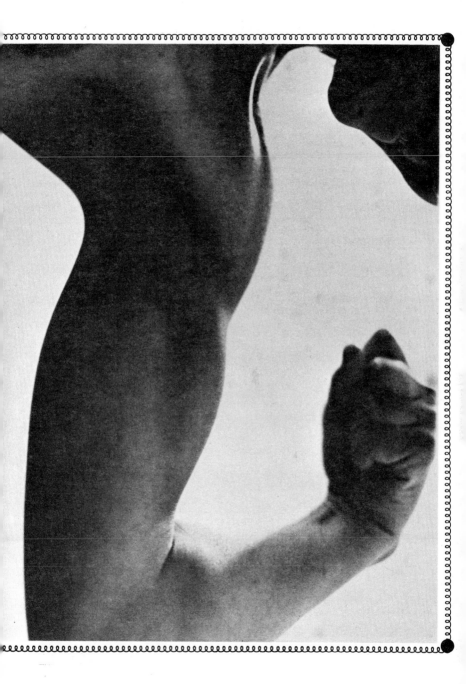

Depression

I toy with birth in December
a false pregnancy
the reality of winter
returns
I am still growing
still needing
but my earth stands neutered
unseeing

I cannot waken her
even to listen

Planting Strawberries

The orgasm comes slowly
I finger your life lines
I separate your roots

      Sturdy Sister

You grow your red fetus
in the shape of my heart

Relationship I

Before splitting

history becomes only remembrances of
pain our memories repeat
screaming screaming
guilty
guilty
guilty

our softness beneath
chaffed by what we
can not be
wearing away
all the reasons

reworked and reworked words
ugly as dry salted streets
Love craving quiet snow
blessed nothing
numbness to feeling

Relationship II

There is a peace here
falling snow
catching on the pines
and holding

each white star
on our mittens
a mystery of self
vulnerable
breathtaking

We touch hands eyes
in awe
needing
accepting a gift of selves
we do not own
can not change

Clay

My pots are hand built
rolled into long loving snakes

held together by thumbmarks

Wood

twisted branches
my fingers feeling for the grain

oiled and rubbed
their heartwood glowing

their history naked
unafraid

Songs Of Stones And Feathers

holding stone
I found you on the beach

fondled and slapped
from your blue sea
your beautiful colors
hidden
whitened
by harsh light

pocked and cracked
sculpted with use
you lie curved inside my palm
like a fetus of my womb

you fit
into my cheek's hollow
still tasting of salt

The stone and I
formed by sea fingers
control in every wave

afraid
to touch my own body
my hands gave
to the back of my cat
the gentleness due myself

this joyous moon
telling stories to my skin
beginning a new diary
loving myself

revering life
as I do
I touch

        my own soft breast
        in awe

to love a woman
soft cheek
her breast in the moonlight

        earth on my heart
        the wonder aching

before
plucking my own breast
feather by feather

        creating wings
        for children

now
tracking my blood
to the top of a mountain

        my wing tips a marvel
        soaring beyond stones

Power w/no hate
no tyranny

Just Power